JOHN B. KEANE is one of Ireland's most humorous authors and is recognised as a major Irish playwright. He has written many bestsellers including *Letters of a Successful TD, Letters of an Irish Parish Priest, Letters of an Irish Publican, Letters of a Matchmaker, Letters of a Love-Hungry Farmer, The Gentle Art of Matchmaking, Irish Short Stories, More Irish Short Stories, The Bodhrán Makers* and *Man of the Triple Name.* His plays include *The Field, Big Maggie, Sive, Sharon's Grave, Many Young Men of Twenty, The Man from Clare, Moll, The Change in Mame Fadden, Values, The Crazy Wall* and *The Buds of Ballybunion.*

THE YEAR OF THE HIKER

John B. Keane

New Revised Text
edited by
Ben Barnes

THE MERCIER PRESS

The Mercier Press
PO Box No. 5, 5 French Church Street,
24 Lower Abbey Street, Dublin 1

© John B. Keane, 1991

ISBN 0 85342 965 0

The Year of the Hiker is a copyright play and may not be performed without a licence. Application for a licence for amateur performances must be made in advance to The Mercier Press, 4 Bridge Street, Cork. Professional terms may be had from Mr John B. Keane, 37 William Street, Listowel, Co. Kerry.

Printed in Ireland by Colour Books Ltd., Dublin

This book is published with the financial assistance of the Arts Council/ An Chomhairle Ealaíon, Ireland

To Flor Dullea
with gratitude

This revised two-act version of *The Year of the Hiker* was first presented by Groundwork in association with Gaiety Entertainments at the Gaiety Theatre on 17 July 1990. The producers would like to acknowledge the assistance of Phyllis Ryan in mounting this revival.

Freda	Stella McCusker
Simey Lacey	Darragh Kelly
Mary Lacey	Noirin Hennessy
Kate Lacey	Joan Brosnan Walsh
Joe Lacey	Brendan Gleeson
Hiker Lacey	Mick Lally
Willie Dolly	Ronan Smith

Director Ben Barnes
Producer Arthur Lappin
Designer Wendy Shea
Lighting Conleth White

Executive Producer Ronan Smith

The Year of the Hiker received its premier by the Southern Theatre Group at the Father Matthew Hall, Cork, on Wednesday, 17 July 1963.

Freda	Mairín Morrish
Simey Lacey	Michael Twomey
Kate Lacey	Kay Healy
Joe Lacey	Flor Dullea
Mary Lacey	Loretto McNamara
Hiker Lacey	James N. Healy
Willie Dolly	Ber Power

Production Dan Donovan

Set Frank Sanquest

ACT ONE

Scene 1

Action takes place in the kitchen of the Lacey farmhouse. The time is the early 1960s, the morning of a September day. There is much bustle and activity as the daughter of the house Mary, is getting married this morning. In the kitchen Freda (sister to the woman of the house) busily sets the table for a brief tea. Fiftyish, she is austere and capable. She goes to the door and calls off.

Freda	Simey will you hurry up.
Simey	Quick as I can.
Freda	Where's Joe?
Simey	Over in the long meadow.
Freda	He'll be late. You'll all be late and Mary will be disgraced.
Simey	*(Entering)* She won't be disgraced. It's a bride's privilege to be late. Tradition – like CIE.
Freda	What!
Simey	The only time they're in time is when you're late.

(He takes off his wellingtons and has his trousers tucked into a jazzy pair of socks)

Freda	What in the name of God are you blathering about?
Simey	Bride's being late at the Church. Keep the husband waiting. It's the first blow to keep the poor old divil in his place.
Freda	Simey! That's not a nice thing to say about your sister.
Simey	*(Laughing)* Aunt Freda, me love, I'm only pulling your leg.
Freda	All right so, but ...

(A cry from upstairs)

Mary	*(Off)* Mother! Mother!
Freda	My God, what's wrong?
Simey	Calm down; she's only burst her suspender belt or something.
Kate	*(Off)* What is it?
Mary	Oh my stockings – they're laddered.
Freda	Be quiet!
Mary	*(Off)* What am I going to do? Freda, Freda!
Simey	Here she comes. Run for cover!

(Mary enters downstairs in her slip. She is nervous and near crying)

Mary	Freda my stockings! What'll I do?
Simey	Wear mine, they'll cause a sensation.
Mary	*(Angry)* Simey!
Freda	It's all right love. I'll ...

(Kate enters to stairs. She is not fully dressed either and starts to take off her stockings.)

Kate	Here Mary you can have mine. I'm not used to these nylon things anyway.
Mary	*(Peeling off a stocking)* They won't fit, they won't fit.

(As they are taking off their stockings, Simey looks from one to the other.)

Simey	This is no place for a parson's daughter.

(He covers his eyes)

Kate	Don't be disrespectful.
Freda	Will you all be quiet for a minute. I thought something like this might happen but it was your mother I expected to make a mess of hers, not you. Mary upstairs in my drawer there's two pairs of new nylons.
Mary	Thanks Freda, you're a life-saver.

(She dashes to Freda, then off).

Kate You think of everything Freda. Hurry now Mary. And you too Simey. And tell Joe to hurry.

(Exit)

Simey You're a marvel Freda. Hey, what were you going to do with the stockings if no one needed them?

Freda Give them to Mary anyway.

Simey You weren't thinking of wearing them to Mass on Sunday and catching the eye of a strong farmer who knows a shapely bit of leg when he sees it? You won't make much impression with the passion-killers you're wearing now.

Freda That's enough of your cheek.

(Takes tea pot and scalds it)

Simey Don't tell me you're giving us a breakfast before we go!

Freda Nothing but a cup of tea.

Simey Good! I don't want my appetite impaired today.

Freda You'd better hurry or they'll start without you. Your clothes are laid out.

Simey Aunt Freda!

Freda What now?

Simey Any chance of the loan of a few quid? You'll get it back.

Freda No chance at all!

Simey Whatsoever?

Freda	None!
Simey	All my mother gave me was a pound. A pound, imagine, for a man of my morals!
Freda	You keep away from the drink today. Your mother mightn't know but I know and I might get it into my head to tell Joe too.
Simey	Don't tell Joe. There's no need for that.
Freda	I will if I find out you're overdoing it again. I taped you well the first time. When a fellow of your age starts eating peppermints, the jig is up!
Simey	A pint....a pint was all I had, and that was just to be sociable.
Freda	Who're you trying to cod? You had a gallon look in your eyes.
Simey	Well, it won't happen again. A pint is my limit from now on, and it isn't for the sake of the drink, you know....
Freda	*(And she concludes the sentence with him)* but for the love of the company..... Well, it better not happen again!

(Enter Kate)

Kate	Good God, Simey! Are you not changed yet?
Simey	I'm just going Ma. I won't be a minute when I get started.... Ma, you wouldn't by any chance consider parting with another pound, would you?
Kate	I gave you a pound last night! I can't imagine what you'd want the second pound for?

Simey	Every car needs a spare wheel!
Kate	A pound is plenty for you Simey. You're costing enough as it is.
Simey	Ah, but I'll be finished after Christmas ...... a qualified horse doctor with money to burn.
Freda	Thank God I'm not a horse!
Simey	*(Without venom, moving towards the other exit)* You mightn't be a horse but you'd pass in a herd.

(Exit Simey)

Freda	There's a lot of his father in that fellow!
Kate	Tie the buttons on the back of this blouse for me. Freda, do you think the day will hold fine?

(Freda ties buttons)

Freda	The minute I made mention of his Da, you changed the subject.
Kate	I changed the subject because I wanted the buttons tied and I haven't all day. I've a daughter getting married you know!
Freda	And you're thinking that if her father was a proper father he'd be here and thanking God that he doesn't know about it, wherever he is, because maybe he might face home and spoil the day for Mary.
Kate	I wasn't thinking of that!
Freda	Are you telling me you didn't think about him at

all today?

Kate   Of course I thought about him today. He's the father of my children and he was my husband for eight years.

Freda   And he wasn't your husband for twenty years.

Kate   Here I am, gabbing and prattling, when I should be above with Mary. She's a bundle of nerves. Freda, don't ever get married!

(Exit Kate)

Freda   Married ... to a man ..... Waugh! *(She makes as if to vomit).*

(A tractor pulls into the yard and stops)

Kate   *(Off)* There's Joe, Freda. Tell him to hurry up.

Freda   *(At oven)* Joe, come on. You'll be late.

Joe   *(In the porch)* There was a ewe in a ditch. I had to pull her out.

Simey   *(Off – Banging on door)* Will you be in there all day, Mary? I want to shave.

Mary   I can't be any quicker.

Kate   Leave the girl alone Simey. She's doing her best.

Simey   *(Entering)* Well for God's sake, she's been in there since the crack of dawn.

(A row breaks out)

Freda	*(To Simey)* Your boots. *(Indicates that he should put them away)*

(Joe rushes in)

Joe	Is that the time? I have to shave.
Simey	*(Coming down stairs)* You won't get into the bathroom. Mary's in there for life.
Joe	What'll I do?
Simey	Join the queue.
Mary	*(Off)* All right, Simey. I'm finished in here.
Simey	And about time.
Joe	Thanks Mary!

(He dashes past Simey and exits. Simey follows shouting. We hear the bathroom door slam. Simey shouts 'Louser'. Freda scalds the teapot and empties outdoor. She starts to sing Red Sails in the Sunset. *As Simey enters, she stops)*

Simey	Go on!.... Go on! ...... a nice slow waltz that .... close dancing, low lights ... a big blonde, or even a small blonde.... *(Falsetto)* 'Do you love me, Gertie?' .... 'To distraction, Samuel!' ...... 'Run away with me, Gertie?'.... 'But I can't, darling, I've got my dancing shoes on!' .... *(Reverts to normal)* Give me some hot water Freda, Joe's in the bathroom. I can't get in.
Freda	If you shaved early this morning, like I told you,

you wouldn't be rushing now.

(Freda fetches kettle and pours water into basin)

Simey   Sure then you'd have no one to give out to. *(Exits to fetch razor and returns)*

Freda   *(Not without affection)* Shave and shut up, you big clown.

Simey   When I have money Freda, I'll stop shaving and grow a beard like Mephistopheles.

(Simey applies lather and commences to shave)

Simey   Is Mary in love with Willie, do you think?

Freda   Of course she is! Why do you think she's marrying him?

Simey   He's a doctor.

Freda   If you turn out half as good as Willie, you'll be all right.

Simey   Do you like Willie, Freda?

Freda   He'll suit Mary.

Simey   Not as dashing as me though!

Freda   When you propose to a sensible girl, you'll find out how dashing you are.

Simey   Did anyone ever propose to you Freda?

Freda   I could have been married, if that's what you mean. A healthy, respectable farmer from Kiskeam was mad about me.

Simey: And what happened?

Freda   Nothing happened! I just wouldn't marry him. I saw enough of marriage in my time. Too much of it to want any part of it.

Simey   Ah, we're back to my Da! What did he run away from? From responsibility? From you Freda?

Freda   If you don't hurry up and shave, you'll be left behind.

Simey   Sure where's the crack if your not coming?

Freda   Somebody has to mind the house. Do you want us to be robbed.. and what about the cows? Will they work the milking-machine themselves?

Simey   Freda.... you remember my father well. What kind of a fellow was he?.... Was he just the lousy bum I think he was?

Freda   He was a wanderer born and bred. We were often at the height of the harvest here and if he heard of a coursing meeting or a football match he was gone. God only knew when he'd show up then. I remember once, the hay was down in the big meadow and your mother was carrying Mary.... he went off to a race-meeting in Mallow and didn't come back for four days.

Simey   No explanation for it?

Freda   He was no good!

Simey   How did you get on with him?

Freda   I couldn't stand him and he couldn't stand me. He broke our hearts. He was always breaking our hearts.

Simey   Whose heart?

Freda   He was all life and bustle. That was the Hiker. He'd wear a person out, he was that full of whims. He was always going – moving, moving. He couldn't sit by the fire and smoke his pipe like a sensible man. You could never depend on him – not for anything.

Simey   Strange!

Freda   Try to picture a man the exact opposite of your brother Joe and you have him. He'd leave here three days before a big hurling game in Dublin and walk the whole way in stages. That's how they gave him the name of 'The Hiker'.

Simey   You didn't like him?

Freda   *(Laughs grimly)* I hated him!

Simey   Maybe that's why he left. I mean if my mother hated him and you hated him.

Freda   We didn't hate him at first.

Simey   *(Sarcasm)* Maybe if there was more understanding....

Freda   Don't make me laugh! He wasn't born to stay in one place. There are others like him. It's in the blood ..... No sense of responsibility, wife and family all forgotten when the humour catches them. Wandering is God's greatest curse!

Simey   Well, you can't blame him so! The thing was in him and he couldn't do much about it.

Freda   Can you forgive a man leaving his wife and children for twenty years..... never once coming back or enquiring if they were dead of alive. You

17

were only a child Simey. You don't know how hard things were until Joe grew up.

Simey Maybe he's dead!

Freda I wish to God he was but if he was we'd have heard of it. No, he's not dead. There are good men gone before their time but never the likes of him.

(Enter Joe, shaved and spruce! He carries the coat of a new suit across his arm, and a tie in his hand. He is a big man, strong, in his prime).

Joe Put this tie on me Aunt Freda and don't go putting one of those new knots on it.

Simey *(Surveys it)* Nice cut! Good bit of material too. What do you think of mine. Of course, I haven't the coat on yet.

Joe I like the shade.

Simey: Yes, conservative, isn't it? Sort of professional tinge to it. Should impress the farmers. All I want now is a waistcoat and a couple of fountain-pens.

(Kate appears on stairs)

Kate Are you not dressed yet? You'll have us all late.

Simey I've me trousers on – I'm decent.

Kate Now, Simey –

Simey It's all right, Mother – I've only my tie and jacket to slip on.

18

Kate	Joe, let me look at you .... turn around.
Joe	Ah God Mother, I'm grand.
Kate	Turn around.
Joe	Ah Mother.
Kate	Do as you're told.
Joe	*(Doing so, muttering)* Jaysus.
Kate	*(Pulls at the back of his jacket)* It's not hanging very well. If I'd time I'd make a job of it.
Joe	It's all right Ma. *(Turning)*
Kate	And look at your tie. God knows, men are the worst hands at making a tie.
Joe	Ha – ha. 'Twas Freda made this knot for me.
Kate	That's what I say – it takes a woman's hand. Now you know what to do when you're giving Mary away?
Joe	Didn't we rehearse it six times last night Mother?
Kate	I'm sorry Joe – you look very fine Joe, and I'm proud of you – but you shouldn't have to give my daughter away at her wedding.....

(Kate exits)

Simey	First year I was at the Uni. there was a fellow from Cobh doing medicine.'Lacey! You wouldn't be anything to the immortal Hiker Lacey that walked across the world and left his wife without as much as a goodbye?' 'He's my father!' I said. The poor fellow nearly dropped dead with fright when I told him. Treated me with tremendous

respect after that. They have a kind of sneaking regard for him in a lot of places.

Joe The same as they have for Cromwell and Jack the Ripper.

Simey Do you know they measure time by the Hiker. I heard two old men at the Creamery one morning. They were talking about a pony. 'When did you buy him?' one old man said to the other. ''Tis a long bit ago. 'Twas about ten years after the Hiker left.' ..... I wonder, does he ever think about us?

Joe Twenty years and not even a bloody Christmas card.

Simey Suppose he came back Joe ....just suppose .....?

Joe I'd break his bloody back.

Simey I don't suppose I'd talk to him. I don't think I could strike him though. His being my father wouldn't stop me. I just couldn't be bothered.

Joe You would if you remembered my mother the first few years after he was gone.

Freda *(Off)* Is there enough petrol in the car Joe?...... Joe?

Simey Yes, I checked it.

Joe *(To Simey)* You remember the Driscoll girl from Fallamore that I used to knock around with?

Simey I do well ...... the dark-haired one. *(To Freda)* Lovely long legs.

Joe You remember when I stopped seeing her? You used to cod me about it.

Simey Yes.

Joe That codding hurt boy, because I was fond of that girl.

Simey Sorry Joe! *(Pause)* What happened?

Joe The Hiker!

Simey Come again!

Joe I called to her house one night to take her to a dance. 'I'm going out with you no more Joe,' she said. 'Is it true,' she said, 'that the Hiker Lacey is your father?' 'I'm his son,' I said. 'Goodbye Joe'.

Simey If that's all she cared for you, maybe you're as well off without her.

Joe That's a hell of a lot of compensation.

(Enter Freda)

Freda Are you going to stay gassing there all day?

Joe No more talk of him now .... This is Mary's day and nothing is going to happen this morning to spoil her happiness ... nothing! Come on now.

Simey I'd better get my coat on.

Joe Did you check the car again?

Simey Yes ..... everything's in order.

Joe What about the spare?

Simey: Perfect.

Joe It's just the kind of morning we'd get a puncture.

Simey Don't worry! Everything will be OK.

Joe You'd think 'twas myself was getting married, I'm that nervous. I wish it was over. Go on and get

21

into your clothes man, and tell the women to
hurry it up.

Simey   (*Exiting*) In parts of Borneo there's no such thing
as marriage. A couple of bags of bulls' eyes or a
quarter-stone of brown sugar and you take what
you want.

(Exit Simey)

Freda   *(Shaking her head)* That fella!

(Freda goes to cabinet and locates a clothes brush)

Freda   Turn around!

Joe   Me mother had me in the parade ring already –
isn't that enough?

Freda   Do what you're told.

(Joe obeys her. She brushes the back of his coat).

Freda   Simey wanted the loan of a pound from me
before you came down.

Joe   And he tapped me for a pound!

Freda   And you gave it to him?

Joe   Ah well, he'll have his own money soon, and
'tisn't every day one of us gets married.

Freda   Do you want a few pounds yourself?

Joe   No! I've plenty! ...... We'll miss Mary!

Freda   'Tis the talk I'll miss. She was always chattering.

Joe	A young woman's talk is better than music around a house.
Freda	She's making a good marriage.
Joe	Aye, Willie's a sound man. You'll be able to manage today, won't you?
Freda	I managed before, didn't I?
Joe	Sorry, I was forgetting. The pig feed is all laid out for you. You can give the blue cow's milk to the calves and you want to watch the tinkers' ponies. We don't want anything getting into the corn. I might start cuttin' tomorrow morning if the weather holds. When you're drivin' in the cows, watch the dogs. Keep them under control.
Freda	Don't worry. The way you've this farm laid out, it runs itself.
Joe	I know! I know! But you can't relax on a farm.
Freda:	'Tis all your doing, you know.
Joe	What is?
Freda	The way we are today. The land in good order and the best of stock. Mary marrying a doctor and Simey nearly qualified. We'd be paupers only for you.
Joe	I only did what had to be done.
Freda	You did more than that! When you should be out enjoying yourself like other young men, you were slaving here.
Joe	I enjoyed it ..... good land is half the battle.

(Enter Simey, spruced and fully dressed)

Simey   They're coming! They're coming! And wait till you see her! Man, she's a real dazzler!

(Enter Kate, followed by Mary. Mary is wearing her white bridal gown and veil. She pauses, upon entering, to be admired. Simey sings: 'Here comes the Bride all dressed in white....')

Mary   Well, will one of you say something? How do I look?
Joe   Out of this world!
Simey   Ravishing!
Freda   You're like something out of a magazine! Come on now, a quick cup of tea.

(Kate bursts into tears)

Kate   Her last under this roof!
Mary   Oh, for heaven's sake Mother! You'd swear I was going to America ....Give me a fag Simey. I have the heebie-jeebies.
Simey   Her last under this roof.
Mary   I can't have tea anyway. I'm fasting.

(Simey hands her a cigarette and lights it for her)

Simey   You can still back out of it. I'll tell him you pulled a muscle getting on your dress.

Mary	Oh, would you Simey, and I can go back to bed again.
Freda	Mocking is catching!
Mary	Do I look all right Freda?
Freda	You look perfect. Wait till he sees you.
Mary	I hope he isn't late or held up or anything. Wouldn't it be awful if we were there first?
Joe	We're late as it is.
Freda	Finish your cigarette Mary. There's no hurry.
Kate	Are we forgetting anything?
Joe	No! .... I'll take the bags out. Come on Simey! Come on man!

(Joe and Simey exit to fetch the bags)

Freda	It's a lovely morning for a wedding. I hope the weather holds up for the honeymoon.
Mary	I suppose I'd better tell *somebody* where we're going, but don't tell the boys. You know what Simey is.
Kate	Rome?
Mary	No.
Freda	Lourdes?
Mary	No! .... we're going to Spain. Willie always wanted to go there.
Kate	How long?
Mary	I don't know for sure. A month at the most. I'm so excited. Were you excited, Mother? .... Oops! .... I'm sorry!

Kate   *(Crying)* Oh, my poor baby ... my little baby...

(Mary goes to her mother and comforts her)

Freda   I won't be a minute.

(Exit)

Mary   I'm sorry for what I said Ma – about your wedding day. I'm so excited I didn't think. I'm sorry!

Kate   It's all right love. Willie is a good boy. He'll be a good husband.

Mary   He will Ma, I know he will. If I wasn't sure of that I wouldn't be marrying him. Poor Ma, it must have been awful for you.

Kate   Not my wedding day, but later on ... Twenty years, and every night of those twenty years that I heard a strange sound I sat up in bed thinking it might be him.

Mary   And pleased it wasn't.

Kate   Not at first. I'd have welcomed him then because I missed him the way you'd miss the beating of your heart. When he didn't come back I grew to hate him but the hate went too after a few years and now it doesn't matter any more. I'm glad he isn't here now, for your sake.

Mary   *(Intensely)* And I'm glad, for both our sakes.

(Enter Freda with a gift for Mary)

Mary   Oh, thank you Freda.

(She starts to cry. Affected, so do Freda and Kate. Enter Simey and Joe. Simey puts cases down and pretends to burst into tears)

Joe   Come on! .... Come on! .....

Simey   But I can't! My make-up is ruined!

(Joe and Simey exit with the bags, but not before Simey gives another yowling cry.)

Mary   This is definitely my last time getting married. You take this for me Mother. I want to take one last look around.

Kate   Her last look around!

(Kate cries again, and exits, dabbing at her eyes and sniffing)

Mary   I wanted a minute alone with you Aunt Freda before I left.

Freda   You'd better go now. Time's moving on. He won't wait for ever. *(She turns aside a little)*

Mary   I want to thank you Aunt Freda, fo everything; for all the nice things you've done for me.

Freda   You'll be late for sure if you don't hurry.

Mary Everything has gone right for me. I couldn't say this to my mother but I had an awful fear my father would show up. Willie knows all about him but his people aren't sure yet. I prayed he was dead. Terrible things to be saying about my father!

Freda Not about *him!* You could be dead yourself, for all he cared.

Mary I couldn't have gone through with it if he'd shown up.

Freda Nonsense! This is the happiest day of your life and don't you forget it. Don't look back. Look forward, because this is the day your life should really begin. Start it smiling and you'll never stop smiling.

Mary Oh Freda ... One thing! ... There's Joe make him go out. Send him away on holidays and send him out nights. He's buried in the land and he'll be old before he knows it.

Freda Joe will be all right. There's something good in store for Joe. Wait and see.

(Enter Simey)

Simey Don't hurry! Don't hurry! I just came in to tell ye that we're only ten minutes late. Personally speaking, I don't mind, but then, of course, I'm not getting married this morning.

Mary Oh, good God! I never realised it was so late. 'Bye Aunt Freda ....thanks for everything!

(Exit Mary. Freda immediately dabs her eyes)

Simey I always say there's nothing like a good cry. I'm sorry I can't join you Freda.

Freda She's all I have!

Simey But you've me .... look at me ..... aren't you glad?

(Aunt Freda cries again and dabs her eyes)

Simey Well, I'll have to be off, and listen Freda .... don't look so lonely. Your turn will come too.

(Exit Simey, laughing)

Freda My turn is gone! I lost my place in the line, rearing another woman's family. *(Sound of car starting and moving off)*

End of Scene 1

Scene 2

(Freda is filling the second of two hot water bottles. A dog barks some way off and is quiet. She corks the bottle and moves towards the stairs. The dog barks again and she turns back, a little puzzled).

Freda   That'll be a fox.

> *She exits upstairs. There is a pause and the Hiker enters. He looks around the kitchen, sees Joe's overcoat hanging on a peg, takes it down and acknowledges the size of the wearer. He puts it back as he hears Freda returning. She stops on the stairs when she sees him).*

Freda   Sweet Jesus! Who are you? Don't come near me. Stay where you are. What do you want? *(She looks at him closely)* It's not you – oh dear God. *(She comes down quickly).* What brought you back, you're not wanted here. You'll have to move on quickly before anyone sees you. If it's money you want I'll give it to you, but you'll have to go.

Hiker   Where's Kate?

Freda   Twenty years we had without you. Keep moving
now and leave us in peace.

Hiker   Where's Kate, I said? Where are they all?

Freda   What's it to you, you're a stranger here.

Hiker   Is she still alive?

Freda   I refuse to answer you, you've no right to ask.

Hiker   *(Threateningly)* Aren't you going to tell me
anything about my family?

Freda   They're not your family anymore. Don't you
understand that? You don't belong here.

Hiker   Belong or not I'm here now. I've come a long way
to find out about my family – twenty-five miles
today itself I walked and my feet in blisters with
the roads. *(With a hint of pleading)* So you better
tell me about Kate and the children.

Freda   If I tell you, will you go?

Hiker   *(With a flash of his old self)* If you don't tell me, I
won't go. Now how is Kate?

Freda   She's well.

Hiker   *(After a pause)* That's not enough Freda, you'll
have to tell me more. Where is she? Where are
they all? ....

Freda   You needn't try to bully me.

Hiker   What are you afraid of? That I'll stop here and be a
cuckoo in the nest you've clucked over all these years?

Freda   And how would they have got on without me?

Hiker   We never had a chance to find out. Now you
better tell me where they are.

Freda   All right. They're at a wedding – Mary's wedding.

Hiker	Máry – the baby?
Freda	Mary is twenty-one years of age. She was married this morning.
Hiker	A car passed me on the road – a wedding party. Think of it, if one of them had stopped to give me a lift –
Freda	Thank God none of them stopped. If you had shown up Mary wouldn't have married. She told me. She has no time for you.
Hiker	Good God! Why?
Freda	Can't you understand, they're ashamed of you. The very mention of your name and they start hating you. Have you forgotten? You left your wife and your little children, walked out on them, hiked off over the hills and far away – went down the road for a box of fags and didn't come back for twenty years.
Hiker	*(Abruptly)* I know how long it was.
Freda	Do you now?
Hiker	These twenty years weren't a joke for me either. I had my pride and there was no coming back for me. Pride is no virtue but pride can give a man a bit of dignity.
Freda	Pride –
Hiker	Yes pride, I couldn't make Kate into a woman with you around, with your novenas and your rosaries. There was no peace and fulfilment in our love-making. Holy Mary's like you should be kept a million miles away from love.

32

Freda   How dare you! Get out of here with your dirty talk and if you do this one good thing maybe God will have mercy on you for all the wrong things you've done.

Hiker   Arrah, let me alone. Your God and my God are different people. They have a nodding acquaintance but that's as far as it goes.

Freda   *(Coming close to him)* You're not going to stay in this house and talk that sort of talk.

Hiker   Don't come too close – the smell of sulphur might gas you.

Freda   I'm warning you, when Joe or Simey come back they won't stand for your nonsense.

Hiker   I'll take my chance with my sons.

Freda   Your sons don't know you. They don't remember you.

Hiker   They're still my sons.

Freda   Is it trying to fool me you are? Or fool yourself? Is it a welcome mat you expect in the door before you? You're like an oul' tom-cat that was out all night coming back in the morning for his milk. Twenty years of lechery behind you and now you want to put your feet up.

Hiker   *(He is stung, but he keeps up the front. With a laugh)* Begob Freda, words of abuse still come easy to you. You haven't changed a bit.

Freda   And you have, I suppose? Is that it? Twenty years of neglect is to be forgotten and we'll start again where we left off.

Hiker You'd never know – we might. Or I might rob the house when your back is turned and go my way again.

Freda Your jokes won't work anymore, me bucko. In the old days you could get out of anything with a joke for the children and a kiss for Kate.

Hiker And a bit of a smile for you Freda, when you were spying on me and Kate together.

Freda Blast you. Get out, get on your way.

Hiker I got out once before – but I wasn't the one should have gone.

Freda *(Challenging)* Who then?

Hiker Turn your mind back. Who hung on when Kate and me were young together, trying to find one another in the first days of our marriage? Who was there every time I turned to Kate? Who sat by the fire when we should have been alone? Who stalked our love till the bed-springs were silent in guilt? ..... You know well, the one who should have gone.

Freda I'd have gone, gone at once, if Kate had spoken.

Hiker Kate was a mouse. I married into this place, I wasn't sure of myself. I was the one should have told you to get out.

Freda You hadn't the right.

Hiker I had every right. I was Kate's husband. No one should be allowed to do what you did – you were like a corpse between the warm bodies of two young people in love.

34

(There is a pause. Freda is not quelled)

Freda	Is this the rhyme you taught yourself by heart in twenty years of running away? Is this the story you told to this one and that when you were looking for sympathy and a drink on the road? Pub talk, me boyo. Singing a song for a few whiskeys and then moaning your tale of woe.
Hiker	What the hell –
Freda	And did they believe you? The ones who stood you a few drinks to be diverted for an hour, the way you pay at a circus to look at the freaks. Of course they didn't believe you; they laughed when you turned away and forgot you for the dirty tramp you are.
Hiker	You know it all Freda, don't you.
Freda	I know you for a liar and a deserter. Well, I've heard your tale and I don't believe you either. There's no free drink for you here but I'll give you a few bob and you can get on your way.

(He watches silently as she gets money and offers it to him)

Hiker	You can keep it.
Freda	Don't be a fool –
Hiker	I'm staying.
Freda	What !
Hiker	I'll stay till my family and my wife come home.

Freda   You can't –

Hiker   Who'll stop me – you?

Freda   When they come in Joe will....

Hiker   When they come in, they're in, and I'll see then. After that I might go on, or I might stay for a minute, or a week or a year – or I might stay till I die – and if I stay or go it'll have nothing to do with you. I'm not afraid of you anymore Freda.

Freda   Then I'm warning you, you'll be afraid of Joe –

Hiker   No I won't. I've been away too far and too long to care any more about fear. Fear gets lost in weariness. It's ground to dust in the passing of fruitless years.

Freda   I had a feeling we'd be seeing you one of these days. The frost came early – that was one sign – and the wild duck are landed long ago – another sign. The bushes are black with sloes and the clouds were never so high – all signs of a bad winter. We'll be having the Hiker now one of these days I said to myself. He'll come back to us now when he's too feeble for the road and too old for more of his debauchery. He'll be wanting to rest up now at the end of his days and to be regaling us with his adventures. *(Bitterly)* Well, there's no fatted calf here for you, you merciless wretch. Great God, you had an awful cheek to come back! Twenty years without a word! Get up on your feet now ..... come on!

Hiker   All that's left is a bit of hope .... for
something.........

Freda   *(Softly)* For what?

Hiker   *(Almost speaks, then stops. In a moment he says)* I've
wanted a lot of things these past few years that I
could never have. I've wanted to walk through
the woods below with an easy mind and my
conscience free, I've wanted to feel the moods of
my time, of these late years – to see the brown
flood in the winter and smell the snow in the air
– friendly snow. I've wanted to feel the silences of
the quiet fields .... to feel something .... anything
.... that would keep me in touch with what I once
was. Sit down woman .... I'm staying.

Freda   *(Almost an appeal)* Don't you understand? They
don't want you.

Hiker   I'll have to wait then, won't I, to find out for
myself.

End of Scene 2

Scene 3

(Action takes place as before. The time is the night of a month later. Joe is working on the farm accounts. Simey enters, wearing overcoat and scarf, and carrying an attache case).

Joe   What kept you?

Simey   I was delayed ... Hard to get a lift.

Joe   Better late than never. I suppose you had a few
          pints?

Simey   A few.

Joe   A good few, I'd say.

Simey   When a fellow picks you up, if he asks you to
          have a drink, you don't tell him to go to hell!

Joe   You don't, but you could have had an orange
          juice.

Simey   You could Joe, but I couldn't.

(Simey takes off his overcoat and puts it aside)

Joe   I don't want to sound like an old woman Simey,
          but wait till you're qualified.

Simey   I don't drink regularly – only when I have the

	money and that's not often.
Joe	Ah, I'm not giving it out to you man! You're entitled to your few drinks now and then ... but for your own sake wait until the exam is over. When are you goin' back?
Simey	Monday morning. What time is Mary coming?
Joe	Around one o'clock tomorrow. Did you get a card?
Simey	I got three!
Joe	Same here .... Seville, Madrid and Barcelona... I'll never see those places.
Simey	*(Taking off his coat)* I will some day. They're certainly moving around.
Joe	I wonder where our father and mother went for their honeymoon?
Simey	A day in town and a night in bed!
Joe	And they thought they were extravagant.
Simey	Where's my mother?
Joe	Sitting-room.
Simey:	Cleaning and dusting for the son-in-law's arrival?
Joe	Exactly.
Simey	Where's Aunt Freda?
Joe	Bed.
Simey	Bed?
Joe	She was complaining of a head cold. We made her go for a while. She hasn't been the same since he came.
Simey	Where is he?
Joe	Out in the stable.

Simey	All the time?
Joe	All the time.
Simey	Did he come into the house since?
Joe	No ..... Freda takes his meals out. We rigged up an old bed for him and there's a stove there.
Simey	How is he?
Joe	Are you worried?
Simey	No. Just asking.
Joe	He walks around the farm all day looking at the grass as if he never saw grass before, feeling the hay with his hands and stroking it like 'twas a woman's hair. He doesn't stir at night.
Simey	Does he ever talk to you?
Joe	Never!
Simey	Or look at you?
Joe	He looks at me. I don't look at him.
Simey	That was quite a mauling you gave him that first night.
Joe	Don't tell me you didn't approve.
Simey	Quite frankly, I couldn't care less, but I don't approve of keeping him out in the stable.
Joe	*(Dangerously)* The stable is where he belongs! He stays there.
Simey	That beating was stupid of course. What good did it do?
Joe	It didn't do **me** any good, if that's what you mean.
Simey	Why did you do it? Was there satisfaction in beating him?

Joe   No, there wasn't! I did it because I always promised myself I would. You didn't think I was going to let him get away with it, did you?

Simey   He's not worth hating Joe. Can't you get that into your head. If he fought back, I 'd agree, but he took it like a dog.

Joe   We'd better clear up one thing right now, while you're in the mood.

Simey   What's that?

Joe   Whose side are you on?

Simey   Oh, don't be silly! He means damn-all to me. It's just that I thought ...... it was my opinion that beating him was beside the point, and this idea of keeping him outside in the stable childish.

Joe   *(Annoyed)* Look! ... it wasn't my idea. He went there of his own accord. That's where he wants to be and that's where he stays.

Simey   But what's the point of it?

Joe   What do you mean?

Simey   I think we should send him packing. I'll be a vet in a few months and we can't have it.

Joe   So it's yourself you're thinking about, not him.

Simey   I'm thinking about all of us. I always believed we were an intelligent family. Well, we're not behaving like one.

Joe   Look – if you're so concerned about him, why not do something about it. You've your own room. You've a big bed. Why don't you share it with him? Nobody's stopping you.

Simey	Are you serious?
Joe	I'm serious. Go on out and bring him in.
Simey	Why don't you do it?
Joe	You're the one that's complaining.
Simey	What do you think I am? I don't want the fumes of twenty years' dirt reeking off me. Didn't you smell him?
Joe	All right! All right! That's enough! Now, I want no more criticism of the arrangements here.
Simey	Who the hell do you think you are?
Joe	Shut up!
Simey	Don't order me Joe! Ask me, but don't order me and maybe I'll shut up when I feel like it.
Joe	You shut up this minute or I'll make you!
Simey	Stop it Granda! I'm not a child any more.
Joe	*(Advances threateningly)* Stop it Simey! Don't get me going! I'm warning you.

(Enter Kate)

Kate	Is it yourself Simey? What's the matter?
Joe	Sorry, Ma ... we lost our tempers ... sorry Simey!
Simey	The cause of it all is outside in the stable. It didn't take him long to make his presence felt.
Kate	What did he do Joe?
Joe	Nothing Ma ... Nothing ....

(Joe exits and Simey collects his bag and coat)

Kate	I can't understand it at all, this fighting and arguing.
Simey	It's our Da. We were fighting over our Da. You wouldn't mind if it was even a valuable thing like a shirt button or a shoe-lace but imagine anybody fighting over our Da.
Kate	I'm afraid of Joe when he loses his temper. That night when he hit — *(She stops)*
Simey	You can't even call him by his name, can you?
Kate	He's your father, no matter what you think of him. I didn't like Joe striking him.
Simey	Did you expect Joe to kiss him on both cheeks? He's a stranger, worse than a stranger – we don't want him here.
Kate	No need for fights.
Simey	You're not going soft about him, are you Ma?
Kate	No.
Simey	You don't want him to stay?
Kate	I don't want fighting Simey, that's all I said.
Simey	But him Ma? What about him? He's still hanging around – did you encourage him?
Kate	I never passed a word to him. For long years now there has been peace in this house. I never wanted to see him again.
Simey	Nor any of us. Let him go his way.
Kate	Down the road and never come back.
Simey	Is that how it was the last time?
Kate	A bright morning. Some words between himself and Freda because she interfered in something he

and I were planning – he took his hat and coat and left the door open behind him.

Simey And that was it? *(Pause)* Saves the trouble of shaking hands, I suppose .... Why in the name of God did Joe waste his time hitting him? Wasn't worth it. And he never even tried to defend himself. If that gets out! I thought it might have turned into a good scrap, not that he'd have had a chance against Joe.

Kate That's enough Simey.

Simey Why the hell doesn't he move on? All the neighbours will be talking in no time.

Kate The neighbours have talked for years. I know that better than you. He'll stay a while, like he always did, and then he'll go again.

Simey The sooner the better.

Kate Yes.

(A pause)

Kate *(Crossing to fire and pouring a cup of tea)* I'll bring Freda up a cup of tea before she settles down for the night.

Simey All right Ma, I'll be off soon myself.

Kate I hope you've been working hard Simey, in the college?

Simey Tooth and nail Ma. When I pass by, students stand with wondering gaze and professors doff their hats.

Kate   I'll start a novena all the same, it's no harm being on the safe side.

(Exit Kate Upstairs. Left alone, Simey goes into the parlour and re-emerges with whiskey bottle as the Hiker who has entered calls 'Kate' softly at the parlour door. There is no reply and he turns to go but as he does so Simey's re-entry arrests his departure)

Simey   *(Pause)* Don't you know me? ... Why don't you answer me? ... This is the first time I've spoken to you in twenty years and you ignore me ..... not very good manners, you know!

Hiker   You're Simon, aren't you?

Simey   They call me Simey ... you can too, if you like. D'you know what puzzles me though?

Hiker   What?

Simey   What I should call you ... What would you say to 'Daddy'? ... No, I don't think so ...You don't look like a Daddy ...You're more of a Paw ... Howdy, Paw! ... Or should I call you 'Pops'? ... After all you did pop off once ... still Pop doesn't seem appropriate either. I think I'll call you 'Hiker' ... you're widely known as 'The Hiker' ... I wouldn't say you're affectionately known, but your exploits have attracted a certain amount of attention.

Hiker   You're studyin' to be a vet?

45

Simey	Correct!
Hiker	Do you like it?
Simey	I like animals ... some animals I don't like.
Hiker	I wish you luck. *(Hiker makes to go)*
Simey	Thanks! ... Don't go ... Sit down ... Relax ... What have you been doing with yourself lately ... these past twenty years, I mean? Did you ever think about me ... not the whole family now, mind you, but me, personally – your little boy, Simey?
Hiker	I thought of you ... I remember you well when you were a child.
Simey	I don't remember you. Joe does though ... Joe will never forget you. How's your face, by the way – that was quite a belt he gave you? Why didn't you hit him back? ... Were you frightened?
Hiker	No.
Simey	Why then?

(The Hiker remains silent. Simey changes the subject)

Simey	Tell us about this wandering – where did you go?
Hiker	Everywhere.
Simey	Everywhere? Were you in Mexico?
Hiker	No!
Simey	Japan.
Hiker	No!
Simey	Timbuctoo? Palm Beach? The White House?

Where the blazes did you go? You're going down
in my estimation.

Hiker   Do you give one damn where I was?

(A pause. Simey is somewhat subdued)

Simey   Were you in England?
Hiker   Yes, I was in England.
Simey   Scotland and Wales?
Hiker   Yes.
Simey   But what did you do man?
Hiker   Worked a day, and moved on.
Simey   Worked. Where?
Hiker   Mostly farm labouring, though I was with the
circus for a season.
Simey   A circus! I suppose you were the clown.
Hiker   No. I was never a clown, a fool maybe, but never
a clown.
Simey   Where did you sleep?
Hiker   I slept out in the summer ... sheds and barns
when 'twas cold.
Simey   What was it like ... I mean, what kind of people
did you meet?
Hiker   Met a few fellows like myself.
Simey   And what did you talk about?
Hiker   Where we'd find a day's work; where was good
campin' places or people that wouldn't turn a
hungry man away from the door.
Simey   What else?

Hiker   Cross dogs! Cross dogs were a nuisance. Police that would make a fellow move on. The state of the world.

Simey   And did you form any important conclusions that could be passed on?

Hiker   Nothin' much!

Simey   Nothing at all?

Hiker   A man makes his own hell, or his own heaven. He must learn for himself.

Simey   Not very original, but I'll make a note of it. What about a song!

Hiker   I was never much of a singer.

Simey   Ah but you must! ... You must! ... I want to get a deeper insight into your character, to understand you better. A man is best judged by his songs don't you think?

Hiker   Your mockin' me now.

Simey   *(Mock astonished)* Oh but I'm not ... You really must sing for me.

Hiker   I've only one song. I suppose every man has one song, no matter how big a scoundrel he is. The biggest thieves and cut-throats I met had a song ... strange songs that didn't fit the men who had them. 'Twas like an old man wearing a little girl's ribbons, or a lusty fellow with a child's plaything. When you'd hear of a fellow who died, you'd remember the song he had. 'Twas the song you'd remember. When a fellow died, you'd hear another fellow say: 'He was a good warrant to

48

sing Shenandoah' or 'He was a great man to put over The Red Flag'.

Simey   We digress man! ... We digress ... Your song is what matters. When was the last time you sang it?

Hiker   I'm not sure. It was a good few years ago. 'Twas near the hills of Lammermuir, way up the Mersey. 'Twould have been the Autumn I think. There was a gang of us potato pickin' and when the day was down we built a fire and chipped in for a barrel of cider. There was girls there. Some Irish girls too, I think. They sang and danced. Somebody asked me to sing ... it might have been one of the girls. I was full of cider and the night was gay. I sang a song but my heart was fit to break after singing it and I never sang it since. I used to sing it for your mother. *(He commences to sing* Red Sails in the Sunset *but stops in mid-verse gazing into the distance)*

Simey   What is it old man ... remorse ... conscience ... or the Irish girl you met pickin' potatoes long ago.

Hiker   I never bothered with women.

Simey   Oh come off it, who are you trying to cod? What about the juicy stories around the camp-fire. It wasn't all cross dogs and the state of the world.

Hiker   There was some talk of women but mostly a man kept those things to himself. It wasn't right.

Simey   Not right eh? ... and would you say it was right to leave a wife and children? ... oh, I'm not annoyed! I accept you for what you are, a freak, a bit of a character, a dirty old man who might have a story. You mean damn-all to me.

Hiker I'm your father. You can't change that.

Simey *(Laughs)* Everybody has a father! Judas Iscariot was somebody's father, so was Hitler but, luckily for me, you're not as well-known as those two boyos.

Hiker Do you forgive me?

Simey *(Surprised)* So that's what you came back for.

Hiker I asked you a question, answer it.

Simey I'll put it this way ... You're not my father. I never had a father. When I needed a father, you weren't there. I don't need a father now. I'm talking to you because you're a curiosity. As for forgiving my father, I can't do that because I have no father. Notice how unemotional I am ... how disinterested ... just making casual conversation with an old tramp who might have been my father. 'Tis like asking me to forgive a shadow.

(Kate appears suddenly at the head of the stairs, carrying the cup and saucer. She stops)

Hiker Kate –

(She turns to go)

Simey Leave her alone. Get out.

Hiker I want to speak to you Kate.

50

Simey   *(Going to door)* Come on, or I'll –

Kate   Simey, don't fight!

Hiker   He won't fight, will you, young lad? If there's any
              fighting to be done he'll call his big brother Joe.
              You won't hit me Simey – not because I'm your
              father, nor because your mother tells you not to
              – but because you're afraid I mightn't keep me
              fists to myself like I did with Joe – I might strike
              back.

Kate   Leave the boy alone.

Hiker   It's all right Kate. I'll leave him alone. We had a
              little chat. I know where I stand with him.

Simey   All right then get out.

Hiker   I want a word with you Kate.

Kate   Please –

Hiker   What I have to ask won't take long.

Kate   *(After a moment)* Ask it.

Hiker   Simon leave us alone.

Simey   I will not.

Hiker   For God's sake, I want to talk to your mother –
              to my wife.

Kate   Go upstairs Simey, I might as well get it over now
              as another time.

(Simey goes up the stairs reluctantly)

Hiker   And don't listen on the stairs.

Simey   *(Angrily)* I'll give you five minutes, that's all.

(Exits Simey. Kate sits)

Hiker   This moment has been in my mind for a long time. If there was anything I could do or say to explain ... I came back once. I stood outside there and looked in and the heart was torn out of me. You were here in the kitchen with her – with Freda. 'Twas April and you couldn't hear me with the high wind. Ye looked happy enough, only that I should have been sitting where she was sitting ... I'm sorry Kate, punish me, anything, but talk to me.

Kate   If I spoke to you, I wouldn't stop for days. All I want in the world now is to see you dead and buried where you can bring no more hurt to me or your children.

Hiker   Men will be doing what I did always. They'll quit the comfort of a bed and the joys of a woman. There's men like me that gets the urge for wandering and there's no power in earth or heaven that will pull us back once the callin' cries come from beyond the fields and rivers. Never a day dawned that I didn't feel the pull of the road. I cursed the weakness that drew me away from all that I ever loved.

Kate   Don't make little of me asking me to believe such talk. How could you love a thing and leave it. Tell me you left for money or another woman, I'll understand that – but not ...

Hiker   *(Desperately)* I never thought of another woman. Women were nothing to me.

Kate   Well I know it. I was your woman for a while but even the binding God gave us and the children I bore you meant nothing to you. Get out of my sight and let this be the last talk we'll ever have together.

Hiker   Kate forgive me. From the red roots of my heart, I'm sorry.

Kate   You're no different to what you ever were. You could always find the word to fool people, to win them to your side. God knows, I wondered sometimes if you even knew yourself what you wanted.

Hiker   I'll go away and never see you again, only say some word of forgiveness to me Kate.

(There is a long pause while she controls herself)

Kate   You took my life away from me and froze the love out of me and if I thought that God would take me this instant I could never find it in my heart to forgive you.

Hiker   Don't say that, Kate ...

Kate   You've made me cry again after all these years and you've hurt me again – me that thought nothin' could hurt any more. You expect me to forgive you,*(Increasing in anger)* me that you scorned and shamed, me that you threw aside for another thing, me that was whispered about by neighbours who said I wasn't woman enough to hold on to her man, me of all the women I know that was the only freak, the only failure.

Hiker   No, Kate. No!

Kate   People whispered about me that I was strange and peculiar because my husband left me. He swapped flesh and blood for the road and turned me into a laughing-stock. How could I forgive you – you that stole my pride and mocked my womanhood and left me to wither in my loneliness.

Hiker   I never mocked you, Kate!

Kate   You mocked me the day you left me. You mocked me when you left my bed for another sport. You mock me now most of all by coming back to me when you're spent and old and filthy. Go, go for God's sake, and never let me see you again.

(Enter Freda and Simey)

Freda   What in the name of God is going on? What happened?

Kate   I don't know. I said terrible things. Things I never say.

Freda   Wasn't coming back enough for you? Look what you've done to her now!

Hiker   *(Angrily)* Leave us be, you bitch, you always came between us. Even in our privacy there was your shadow hanging over us.

Freda I never said a word against you.

Hiker And you never said one for me. I should have put you out the minute I came into this house.

(Joe enters through back door, unnoticed)

Freda You'd put me out of my own house would you. I had as much claim to the farm as Kate.

Hiker Why the hell didn't you get married like any woman.

Freda I didn't want to get married.

Hiker Then you should have gone to a convent. In the name of Christ, why didn't you get out and leave us alone?

Freda Would you have me walk the roads like a tramp?

Hiker I'm the one had to do that. *(Wearily)* I'd better go on my way, I'm not wanted here.

Simey How did you guess – or are you still playing for sympathy? Trying to win our pity with a recitation of your wrongs. Poor ill-treated old man, turned out in his old age.

Hiker No.

Joe *(Suddenly)* Get back to the roads you were born to – to the rivers and the ditches and the camp fires. You'll find men like yourself there who'll listen to your tale of woe, and pretend to believe you – but only pretend, because they know that any man who runs away like you did is a liar. You deserted us. You blame Freda for being strong, you blame me mother for being weak, maybe you blame God for making you the way you are – but the truth is, you ran away because things didn't go the way you wanted. Did you ever think of blaming yourself for being a deserter?

Hiker *(Too anxiously)* I did, I did – all these years –

Joe Jesus, can't you tell the truth even with your family?

Hiker *(Facing it at last)* You said 'your family'.

Joe *(After a pause)* I did.

Hiker You didn't speak in kindness but those are words close to a man's heart.

Simey He's off again, the old fake.

Joe Quiet Simey! Let's hear him out – for the last time. Then he goes. *(To Hiker)* Look at our mother. Say your piece and be off. Why did you come back?

Hiker If I tell you about twenty lonely years, you won't believe me. The thoughts of home, of all of you – children's voices making me remember. Longing to come back and pride keeping me away.

Simey Pride?

Hiker Yes pride! Maybe he's right – *(Defences down)* Talk is no good – I wanted to come home.

Joe Beaten – is that how it was?

Hiker Yes.

Freda *(Triumphantly)* I knew it, I said it! A place to put

56

his feet up and die in peace.

(Freda exits with Kate. The Hiker says no more. He rises and moves to the door)

Joe	What else? *(Stopping Hiker at door)*
Hiker	She said it. *(Indicating Freda)*
Joe	Said what?
Hiker	I didn't come here to persecute you. I came home to die.

(Exit)

Simey	The bloody old faker. You don't believe him Joe, do you?
Joe	*(Uncertain)* I don't know.
Simey	My God! I take my hat off to him, he's codded you. Now I suppose we have him for life.

(Simey exits. Joe remains on stage alone)

End of Act One

ACT TWO

SCENE 1

Action as before.
Time is lunch-hour of the following day.
The kitchen table is covered with a starched white linen
tablecloth and upon it reposes the best cutlery and ware. There is
a vase of colourful flowers and a jug of diluted orange in the
centre of the table.
Kate is shining the glasses, which are placed around the table.
Freda is attending to the oven of the cooker, where she is seen to
be ladling gravy over the body of a turkey.

Kate   They're overdue!
Freda   Joe should have gone to pick them up. Don't you
           know Simey won't leave the town without a pint,
           and there's bound to be a celebration when they
           meet.

Kate	How's the turkey coming?
Freda	All right! Another half-hour and he'll be ready. He's a lovely bird.
Kate	'Twas **you** fattened him.
Freda	There's nothing like a good turkey for a homecoming.

(Freda closes the oven door, and attends to a pot on top of the cooker)

Freda	This soup will be spoiled if they don't hurry. Mary was never in time for anything in her life.
Kate	She was once!
Freda	I don't remember it.
Kate	I do ... she was an eight-months birth!
Freda	That's the only time and you're lucky she didn't have any say in it.
Kate	Not even her wedding! But she gets there just the same. I wonder how she'll react to her father?
Freda	She won't react to him at all, because she won't see him.

(Enter Joe)

Joe	No sign of 'em yet?
Kate	No.
Freda	Where's the Hiker?
Joe	I told him to stay away from the house. I didn't like it. This is between myself and Mary. She's

the one to decide. I don't think he'll come near
the house, though.

Freda   Good!

Kate   Let's hope so!

Joe   A strange thing ... I was looking for a winkers in
the car-house this morning and I saw a little
push-cart he made for me. I didn't look at it since
he left. He must have put a lot of work into that.
'Twas a lovely piece of craftsmanship. He must
have spent weeks at it.

Freda   Where's he now?

Joe   He's down at the end of the farm, walking
around the headlands, pickin' up stones and
throwing 'em aside. He sits down every few
minutes. Gives him all he can to stoop down.
He's a goner, I'd say ... I smell turkey!

Kate   It won't be long.

Joe   I'm hungry. I could eat the leg of a pot.

Freda   Be patient and you'll have the leg of a turkey.

Joe   What about a small bit o' stuffin', to take the
edge off my hunger.

Freda   No!

Joe   Ah come on, me oul' darlin! D'you want me to
starve?

Freda   None of your flattery now, my boy. I know you!
If you start eatin', nothing on earth will stop you.

Joe   You're a hard woman Freda. The oul' Hiker is in
a bad way all right. He's a pitiful sight when he
tries to exert himself.

Freda   That's why he came back. He couldn't hike to
the crossroads now. They're all the same. They'll
search the face of the earth for pleasure. The
night is the same as the day to his likes. Twenty
years ago this morning, if there was the rumour
of a cockfight in Fermanagh, he'd be off at
daybreak. He wouldn't even want an overcoat.
But that's all over now. The drive is gone out of
him and the spirit is broken. He smelled the news
of a bad winter, wherever he was, and the
thought of it was too much for him – so he came
back. I knew he'd come back!

Joe   You knew!

Freda   I felt it this autumn. I said it to no one but I
knew it because I know the man.

Joe   Willie and Mary I'm thinkin' about ... and that's
them, now.

Freda   Listen, now! ... Something very important ...
Nobody says a word about him. We'll pretend
that things are as normal as always.

Joe   Things aren't though ... and they both know by
now.

Freda   Granted ... but Mary will twig. Mary will go
along with it, and so will Willie.

Joe   I hope your right! But you know how Simey puts
his foot in things!

Freda   Simey's not that big a fool.

Kate   Mary is very sensitive.

(Enter Simey)

Kate   Well!

Simey   Ladies and gentlemen ... I wish to announce Doctor and Mrs William Dolly, who have just returned from an extended holiday on the Continong!

(Enter a gushing Mary, followed by Willie. Mary immediately rushes to her mother and they embrace. Mary embraces Freda. Joe shakes Willie's hand warmly. Mary embraces Joe. Kate and Freda shake hands with Willie).

Joe   Well, how're they all in Spain?

Willie   The bullfighting was fantastic. Just fantastic! Some of the most incredible sights you ever saw.

Mary   *(To Kate and Freda)* I have lace mantillas for both of you ... hand woven.

(The three women exit temporarily, talking excitedly)

Willie   *(To Joe)* You'd have loved the bullfighting. We actually saw a man being gored. There's nothing to touch it! You can smell the tension before the fight starts, literally smell it. Ha ... toro ... ha ... I'll never forget it. You'd have to see it to believe it.

Joe	It sounds terrific.
Willie	I thought hurling was a game of skill ... but bull-fighting, my God! ... it's the electricity that gets you. I swear I saw flashes in the air before the big events.
Simey	I got a chase from a bull once ...
Willie	Bullfighters are the last of the gladiators ... Ha ... toro! ...

(Simey retreats, tosses his head and snorts like a bull. Willie produces his handkerchief, flaunts it, stands like a matador, stamps his legs and calls: 'Ha ... Toro ... Toro.' Simey charges mildly and Willie easily avoids him.)

Joe	What about a drink Willie?
Simey	A good idea!
Joe	Whiskey or sherry?
Willie	I'll have a sherry. I drank brandy out there at eight shillings a bottle. Good brandy ... eight bob, imagine! One tenth the price I paid for it a month ago last Sunday in the Marina Hotel in Cork city.
Joe	*(To Simey)* Looks like Spain's the place for you Simey. *(He hands sherry to Willie)* Which do you want?
Simey	I'll try a drop o' whiskey. The oul' stomach isn't too good these days.
Willie	Can I help ... no fee!

Simey   No! ... No! ... I know what does me good.

Joe   I could have sworn this bottle was full!

Simey   Evaporation ...

Joe   My foot! *(He pours whiskey for Simey)* I'll have a sherry too, in honour of the occasion. *(Pours himself a sherry)* Well gents, a toast to our new brother-in-law.

(They quaff)

Willie   Joe, you should try to get away sometime ... seriously, I mean .... take a month off. Go to Spain. It's worth it. A man should have one good holiday in his life.

Joe   Maybe on my honeymoon!

Willie   Don't wait for your honeymoon ... Go now!

Joe   Easily said ... what about the farm?

Willie   No matter what you do, the grass will grow. The cows will give milk. The land will still be there when you get back. It doesn't cost much and it's well worth it, believe me. I can think of nobody who needs it more than you.

Joe   I'll think about it, doctor. I couldn't go for a while, though. There's our beloved father ... Did Simey tell you?

Willie   Yeah!

Joe   How did Mary take it?

Willie   *(Shrugs)* Too early to tell. It was a good idea not to tell us during the honeymoon ... could have

64

	spoiled it. What's he like?
Joe	Old ... worn-out ... nothing remarkable about him. You'd expect he'd have some rare quality, something unusual, but he's just like any other old tramp. He doesn't look well to me, not the man he was.
Willie	Want me to have a look at him? *(Unanswered)* If he's bad I could take him off your hands ... put him in a hospital.
Simey	Now, that's a good idea! Why didn't I think of that?
Willie	What do you think Joe?
Joe	I don't know! We'll see. There's no hurry ... He mightn't let you examine him. He doesn't have to, you know.
Simey	I'll rope him up if he won't ... Joe, this is a marvellous chance man. It's just what we need.
Joe	I'll think about it. We won't talk about it now.
Simey	But why not? ... Now's the time! The man is an embarrassment, can't you see that ... an embarrassment for Willie here and for Mary and ... and... me.
Joe	There's no hurry I said. Plenty of time.
Simey	But good God man, this is a godsend!
Joe	*(Angrily)* Not now I said! We'll talk about it some other time.

(There is an uneasy silence, which Willie breaks after a moment)

65

Willie   I heard a damn good story from a Scotsman I met in Barcelona ... honeymooner too. There was this fellow who couldn't smile, see. Went to a Doctor. Doctor told him the skin on his face was too tight. Tough luck on the patient. Went to a second doctor. Same story ... nothing to be done: skin too tight. Went to a quack. Simple, the quack said; just graft a bit of skin from your arse on to your face and you'll be able to grin and bear it at the same time.

(They all laugh)

Simey   I heard one the other night ... a great story. Paddy the Irishman, Paddy the Englishman and Paddy the Scotsman were sleeping in the same bed one night ...

(Enter Mary, coatless, followed by Freda and Kate)

Mary   Sorry gentlemen ... was it a good one Simey?

Joe   Have a drink Mary?

Mary   I'll have a ... Tia Maria? .... A Dubonnet? ... Oh give me a sherry.

(Joe pours a sherry and hands it to her)

Joe   Mother, what about you?

Mary   *(To Kate)* Have a whiskey ... give her a whacker Joe. 'Twill do her good.

(Joe pours a little sherry and hands it to his Mother)

Simey	And Freda ... what about Freda?
Freda	Count me out! The cook has to stay sober. There's enough boozers in the house.
Simey	Yes! .... Disgraceful, isn't it?
Joe	Come on! Don't be a spoilsport! Everybody has a drink. Look, I'm drinkin' a sherry myself.
Mary	Go on Freda. A small dash –

(Mary pours a little sherry, hands it to Freda, forces it upon her. Freda accepts)

Willie	Now, a toast! ... To my in-laws, every one: that they might never need my services.
ALL	Hear! Hear!
Simey	To Doctor William Dolly – bullfighter extraordinary!

(Laughter and more 'Hear! Hear!')

Joe	To the cook, and to the cock-turkey!
Freda	Now, everybody sit down. Soup first!
Mary	I'll help.
Freda	Nobody helps! That's an order.
Joe	Our guest takes the place of honour.
Freda	Anybody who doesn't like turkey, hold up a hand please.

(More laughter. They arrange themselves at the table)

Mary	Spain or no Spain, it's good to be back. There's no place like Ireland.
Joe	When do you start work Willie?
Willie	Tomorrow night. The house is ready too, by the way. Nothing to do but move in.
Joe	I hope you'll both be very happy.
Simey	Same here.
Willie	Thanks Joe! Thanks Simey! ... I know we will ... I've got me a great little wife.
Mary	Don't speak too soon.
Simey	*(Hugs Mary)* Your a lovely little girl aren't you. You're a dote.
Kate	Simey, put that cigarette out!

(Freda takes Willie's plate, fills it with soup and returns it to the table)

Willie	This smells good! It smells like soup. It is soup!

(Freda takes Joe's plate, fills it and places it on the table)

Joe	*(To Simey)* Pass the bread. *(Simey does so)*
Mary	I didn't like the Spanish hair-styles. They have that oily, greasy look.
Willie	That's natural oil.
Mary	How do you know?
Simey	A good question! Make him answer it.

(More Banter)

Willie	*(To Mary)* I was telling Joe he should go to Spain.
Mary	Oh, he must! He must!
Simey	With me as a guide.
Joe	I'd really want a holiday after that.

(Freda places soup in front of Simey)

Simey	I like Spanish women. I believe they get fat shortly after marriage.
Willie	Well, now, that's an absolute fallacy. We met several married women and they weren't fat. As a matter of fact, we didn't see any fat women – did we, sweetheart?
Mary	No .... not that I recall.
Willie	So, you see!
Simey	Yes ... I'll have to find out for myself. Not that I've anything against fat women, or any kind of women.

(Freda places soup in front of Kate)

Joe	A bit of fat is all right ... but not too much of it! Well Willie, what do you think of married life?
Willie	*(Looking fondly at Mary)* There's nothing like it. Every man should marry.
Simey	You hear that Freda? There's still hope for you.
Freda	*(To Simey)* Drink your soup, like a good boy!

Mary	Clothes are cheap in Spain. I bought a sheer silk slip for fifteen shillings and you should see the shirt Willie got for a pound. It takes a while to get used to the food. I couldn't eat it at first ... just couldn't eat it. Some of the things they eat there, you just wouldn't believe it. If I was there forever I couldn't take the food.
Willie	All right when you get used to it though.
Mary	Aren't you going to sit down Aunt Freda?
Kate	Yes Freda ... sit down!
Freda	I'll skip the soup ... I don't feel like it ....

(Willie says Grace)

Joe	The traps are up!
Freda	Eat up now.
Willie	We spent a night in Paris, by the way. *(All echo: 'Paris!')*
Mary	Just a night ... we only had a few hours. I didn't care for it.
Willie	Well, we didn't see much of it.
Simey	What were you doing? When I qualify I'm going to Paris for a week and when I come back I'll make my pronouncement about French women. If I'm able.
Freda	Now does anyone want anymore?
Mary	They don't eat lunch the way we do.
Simey	Nobody does! *(Slooping soup from a spoon. All laugh.)*

*(The door opens and the Hiker enters. He is a little
more spruce than usual. He advances a little way
into the kitchen but as yet nobody notices him. The
conversation goes on. Freda is kneeling at the door of
the cooker, ladling gravy over the turkey).*

Willie Remarkable thing, you can get a good wine in
Madrid for as little as three or four shillings a
bottle. Of course, wine is a necessity there, not a
luxury. They drink it like water.

Joe What's the population of Madrid?

Willie I don't know ... must be over a million .....

*(His voice tails off. He is the first to notice the
Hiker. Then, as if by contagion, there is a silence
and everybody stops eating. Freda, sensing
something, rises and is silent. The Hiker advances a
step towards his daughter who has turned to look at
him. The Hiker looks at her for a long while)*

Mary Somebody change places with me please!
*(She rises immediately. Willie takes her place; she
takes his)*

Mary Why have we stopped eating? Is there something
wrong with the soup? Here's your soup dear. Pass
mine, will you, please.

(Willie does so. Willie looks closely at the Hiker for a

while. The Hiker turns and exits quickly)

Mary	God! I didn't think he would be that bad. Rip Van Winkle is only trotting after him.
Willie	That's a sick man ... a very sick man. I think I should have a word with him while your dishing up Freda.
Mary	No you won't. We'll have our first fight if you do.
Willie	The man is sick and I'm a doctor. *(Goes to exit)*
Simey	What do you think's wrong with him?
Willie	I don't know. That yellow tinge. The yellow in the eyes.
Joe	What is it?
Willie	It could be a lot of things.
Joe	Willie, what is it?
Willie	It looks like cancer of the liver ... very advanced I'd say.

(He exits)

Freda	Who's going to help me carve the turkey.
Simey	Ah, the turkey.

(Kate rises)

Kate	I'll do it. Let the men sit where they are...
Mary	I haven't eaten turkey since Christmas.
Simey	What ... no turkeys in Spain.

Mary   Chickens ... nothing but chickens. And mean little chickens they are. Hardly a pick on some o' them ...
(Joe rises and excuses himself)

Simey   What's the matter with **you**?

Joe   Funny, I'm not hungry anymore. That old reprobate is after putting me off my dinner. I'll get a breath of fresh air.

(Joe goes to door and inhales deeply)

Simey   Keep upwind of the Hiker!

Freda   Sit down Joe, I'll be taking him his dinner in a minute.

(Kate silently, almost unnoticed, leaves the room)

Joe   *(Still looking out of the door)* By God! You wouldn't think he could put us off our dinner like that ... a man that means nothing to us, nothing at all, spoiled the whole bloody thing – for me, anyway.

Simey   Sit down, for heaven's sake, and forget about him! *(Pause)* Now maybe you'll reconsider the hospital. It's only natural. They're equipped for this sort of thing. Everybody goes there to die, sooner of later.

Mary   Simey's right Joe.

73

Joe   There are things I remember about him, small things. The patience he had when he was teaching me how to use a hurley. Often walked five miles to a match with me on his shoulders. Even when he hadn't the money, he'd always manage a lemonade for me. When he came back from one of his hikes he always brought me something. I know what he did to us, as well as any of you, but I think any man should be left pick the place where he wants to die – even a renegade father.

(Exit Joe)

End of Act Two Scene 1

Scene 2

Action takes place as before.
The time is a few weeks later. Late evening.
In the kitchen Joe is soldering a large creamery tank, when
Simey enters, seizes him, and waltzes him around the kitchen.

Joe   What the hell is up with you?

Simey   I got it man! I got it! I'm through!

Joe   The Exam?

Simey   *(Flourishes a telegram which he carries in his hand)*
             I got it! I got it! I'm a vet ... Just happened to
             saunter down to the Cross and this wire was
             waiting for me. Would you believe it, I was afraid
             to open it. I got somebody else to do it ... I passed
             man! ... Aren't you going to congratulate me?
             Look! Read it! *(Reads)*: 'We're through, you bags
             stop. We're through stop. O'Mara stop.'

Joe   I'm delighted ... Congratulations Simey! I'm
             really delighted. I didn't think you'd make it. I
             thought you were squandering your chances up
             in Dublin.

Simey   Ma! Freda! I knew I'd get it all along. I had the
             confidence man.

(Simey emits a loud and joyous yell and cavorts around the kitchen, Freda enters)

Simey Look at me and tell me what you see?

Freda I see the effects of too much porter.

Simey Wrong! ... You see a Vet ... a fully qualified Veterinary Surgeon.

Freda *(Delighted)* You passed?

Simey Of course I passed!

Freda Oh, congratulations Simey!

(She embraces him. Enter Kate)

Kate What's all the commotion about?

Joe He qualified. He got a telegram.

(Kate embraces him and immediately begins to weep)

Freda It's marvellous and all the doubting we had, to think he was slaving away all the time.

Kate 'Twas my prayers ... I promised St Jude ...... We misjudged him. He was working all the time.

Freda Mary must be told. *(To Kate)* Come on we'll get ready and go down to the Cross. We'll put a call through to the hospital and tell Willie. They'll be delighted. Oh, it's simply marvellous. Come on Kate!

(Exit Kate and Freda to get ready and go out)

Simey	This calls for a celebration *(Simey crosses to the parlour)* Simey Lacey BSC, MVB, MRCVS.*(Joe takes the whiskey and pours one for Simey)* Fair play to you.
Joe	Well? What does it feel like?
Simey	I don't know! I'm dizzy! I've waited five years for this day ... but it's worth it, by God. No more bloody books.
Joe	That must be a relief to you.
Simey	A relief? ... It's more than that. For the first time in my life I'm independent. From here on I needn't give a damn about anybody. I can come and go as I please and be responsible to nobody, because if a man has a profession his sins are excusable and if he's a success they like him for his sins. This is what I've always wanted Joe. I have the means of arriving somewhere. I have a vehicle.
Joe	*(Disappointed)* I hope you'll talk to us now and again.
Simey	I'll talk to you now. There's an old house down at the Cross where I could start up. I could buy if for £500. It's a start. There are 300 suppliers at the Cross creamery. That's 300 customers, and if there's a better foundation for a good practice, it's news to me.
Joe	I'll secure you man, you needn't ask. I haven't got

£500 in cash – not after Mary – but my word is good.

Simey   Thanks Joe! I knew you'd see me through to the end. *(Rubs hands)* Now I needn't give a rattlin' damn about anybody ... and I'll marry well too ... I've the qualifications now, better mark than a mere student. I should have no trouble marrying money and less trouble marrying land.

Joe   I could give you a loan of a hundred cash, to start with. It'll be a squeeze, but I'll manage it.

Simey   God that would be great ... great altogether ... there's one other thing!

Joe   What's that?

Simey   The old man. Now give me a chance before you interrupt and let's be practical about him. He hasn't much time and this is no place for a dying man ... now hear me out Joe ... we'll chip in, all of us, and put him in a nursing home. It's better than he deserves. There's no other way out of it.

Joe   No! ... and that's a final no!

Simey   Ah, come off it man. It's the only solution.

Joe   He came home to die. Let him die here. God Almighty, that's not much to ask.

Simey   You can't have him dying here man! The embarrassment of if would be deadly.

Joe   Not for me! ... whatever he's done, he's still my father.

Simey   Look Joe, you'll have to take other people's feelings into account.

Joe   What other people?

Simey   Well mother and Freda and Mary and me.

Joe   Mary isn't here ... My mother and Freda don't mind and I don't mind. You're the only one.

Simey   Well it isn't fair to me!

Joe   How selfish can you be Simey?

Simey   I'm not selfish!

Joe   You've had every chance. You never had to worry about the money for your education. You never had to worry about Mary or my mother or anyone. But I'll say this for you ... you certainly worried about yourself!

Simey   What the hell's the matter with you? ... You've been acting strangely since the Hiker came back. You've a conscience about him Joe ... I haven't. Man, mind thyself, that's my policy.

Joe   Yes ... I can see that.

Simey   What in the name o' God do you want me to do?

Joe   Nothing! Nothing!

Simey   I'm going down to the Cross for a few drinks. I think I'm entitled to them .... or do you disapprove?

(Enter Kate and Freda , wearing coats)

Kate   Were you two arguing again?

Joe   No! ... No! ... There was no argument.

Simey   Yes there was, and he started it. He has an obsession about the Hiker.

Joe	I have not.
Simey	He wants him to stay here. Doesn't want to send him to hospital.
Freda	But I thought it was all fixed up! You told me yourself Simey, that Joe would be for it.
Joe	Nothing is fixed up. Why don't ye let him alone? You've all had your revenge. Isn't it enough to see the poor oul' devil dying? What more do you want?
Simey	We want the obvious ... the hospital is the place for a dying man.
Kate	What do **you** want, Joe?
Joe	I don't know in the hell what I want! In the name o' God, let me alone. What do ye expect from me?
Kate	Nothing Joe, nothing. Do whatever you want. It's all right with us.
Joe	Is it? The thing is that you don't know what you want, any of you. You want me to do everything. Well I'm not doin' anything – d'you hear? I'm not doing one goddam thing about anything. No man ever sat in judgement on his own father. I'm going out. I'm sick of ye. I don't know where I am.

(Exit Joe)

Simey	I can't figure him out.
Kate	Let him alone. That's the best way. Come on

Freda. Joe knows what he's doing.
(*Exit Kate*)

Freda   Simey, let Joe decide about his father. He's the
             boss of the house. No one else has a right.

(*Exit Freda. Simey walks irritably, slapping his fist
against his palm. He then goes to door and calls*)

Simey   Joe! Are you out there, Joe? Come in here a
             minute.

(*There is no reply. Simey turns and stares moodily
into the fire. The Hiker appears in the doorway*)

Hiker   He's gone down to the end field.

Simey   I didn't call you! I called Joe. You've no right to
             appear there, like a bloody ghost.

Hiker   Sorry! ... I only came in to congratulate you on
             your Exam.

Simey   Where were you listening?

Hiker   I couldn't help but hear it. I said I'd come in and
             tell you how glad I was.

Simey   No thanks to you!

Hiker   Sorry!

Simey   Sorry! Sorry! Don't be always so shaggin' sorry!

Hiker   Sorry!

Simey   When are you going to hospital?

Hiker   What?

Simey	*(Shouts)* I said when are you going to hospital?
Hiker	Hospital?
Simey	Hospital – where sick people go to .... where you should be. Didn't you notice yourself disimproving these past weeks? Or have you lost your sense of reasoning as well as your sense of smell?
Hiker	I know what's wrong with me.
Simey	Then why the hell don't you go where you belong?
Hiker	I couldn't go to hospital.
Simey	Why not?
Hiker	I can't leave here.
Simey	You can't.
Hiker	I've only a little while more. I can't leave here now.
Simey	You left before and you had no qualms about it.
Hiker	That was different.
Simey	It wasn't different! You had to go then, hadn't you? ... You had the urge for wandering ... Well you have to go now, too ... I'll fix it. Joe need know nothing about it 'til you're gone.
Hiker	*(Fear)* No man ... no ... you see, I can't go ... I have to stay here. It won't be long. It's all I ask now, to be left stay here. To have someone of my own blood near me, to cross my hands and close my eyes when my life gives out, it's not much to ask.
Simey	You've no right to ask anything.

Hiker	Maybe not, but I can die in spite of **you**!
Simey	Get one thing into your head old man! You're goin' to hospital. That's final.
Hiker	*(Spirit)* I'm not going!
Simey	Oh yes you are!
Hiker	I'm not! You won't make me go. If Joe says so, I'll go. It's whatever Joe says.
Simey	*(Threat – goes near him)* Well I'm sayin' you'll go. This carry on has gone on long enough. I'll beat the daylights out of you if you don't go!
Hiker	I'm not afraid of you! I owe you nothing.
Simey	*(Loudly)* I'm your son amn't I?
Hiker	You feel nothin' for me ... nor for anyone.
Simey	*(Slaps Hiker across face)* Don't talk to me like that! *(Hiker stumbles. With pure hatred Simey shouts)* I'd finish you now if I thought I'd get away with it.
Hiker	I know a coward when I see one.
Simey	*(Shrilly)* Don't tempt me or I'll ....*(He seizes Hiker by the lapels and shakes him. Joe appears in doorway)*
Joe	*(Quietly)* Let him go!

(Simey shakes the Hiker aside in disgust)

Simey	If I catch him in this kitchen again, I'll brain him ...
Joe	*(Quietly)* I thought you said you were going to the Cross?
Simey	When I please! *(To Hiker)* Get out and stay out!

Joe	Stay put!
Simey	Watch it Joe! D'you know what you're doing?
Joe	I do!
Simey	He's going out!
Joe	You have it wrong Simey. **You're** going out.
Simey	What?
Joe	Get out!
Simey	*(Laughs nervously)* You can't bully me! That day is gone!
Joe	*(Slowly)* Don't be too sure! It's costin' you nothing if he stays.
Simey	I'm not a student any more. I don't want people pointing me out as the son of a freak. *(To Joe)* Don't you know that he's all the talk again. 'The Hiker is back!' they say and they have a grudging admiration for him. Well I haven't! I'm clearing out and I won't be back till he's growing daisies and no one talks about him any more.

(Exit Simey)

Joe	He doesn't mean that! He'll be back when he cools off. Simey is all right down deep. A bit of straightening out is all he needs and the world will do that. He'll be back for sure.
Hiker	He won't be back till well after I'm dead. I'm sorry I caused so much trouble .... Good-night, Joe!
Joe	Don't go a while .... How do you feel?

Hiker	It won't be long now.
Joe	In the morning I'll get Willie to have a look at you. Do you want a priest?
Hiker	God knows, I could do with one.
Joe	I'll see to it in the morning. Meanwhile, you'd better sleep here. You can use Mary's old room. It's the nicest room in the house.
Hiker	Why are you doing all this?
Joe	Don't bother me with questions now, but do as you're told.
Hiker	Whatever you say .... I'm sorry Joe, about everything.
Joe	I told you to let things alone.
Hiker	I can't, until you say you forgive me.
Joe	You did me no wrong. You wronged yourself most of all.
Hiker	If that's the case, then say you forgive me.
Joe	I want to make something clear ... I've forgotten what you did ... it's all over. I have nothing against you but you can't expect me to throw my hands around your neck, because that kind of feeling isn't in me. It was before you left. You were God and man rolled into one then. I used to cling to you like a leech. Didn't you understand the way a small boy feels about his father?
Hiker	God! ... I'm sorry Joe.
Joe	Yes ... I know! ... I know!
Hiker	I'm truly sorry.
Joe	*(Anger)* You're sorry ... so you're truly sorry!

What the hell good is that now? You were all I
had. They couldn't give me what I wanted. I
became a sober old man at seven years of age. I
grew up overnight. You took the heart out of me
altogether.

Hiker   Oh God, I'm sorry!

Joe   You're sorry. *(Seizes Hiker by the lapels)* Why the
hell didn't you take me with you? I'd have
followed you to hell because you were my father.
When it dawned on me that you weren't coming
back the hatred built up inside of me. *(Lets him
go. Brokenly)* All you had to do was take me with
you. That was all.

*(Enter Kate and Freda. They both look at the Hiker
in some surprise, and then they look at Joe)*

Joe   He'll be stayin' in the house from now on. (*He
waits for a reply from the women but neither says a
word*) I'll get a doctor and priest in the
morning... I'll go up and throw the bed together
in Mary's room. Mother, you see to the sheets.
There'll be a priest coming.

(Kate exits dutifully)

Joe   I want to hear no arguments from you Freda. Not
a word, you hear? I'm not judging him, so let
nobody in this house judge him.

(Exit Joe)

Hiker	Don't worry yourself! It won't be for long.
Freda	If you're to be here, I can accept that. You'll want a change of clothes for the priest. That's no way to face him!
Hiker	Is it me or you that'll be looking for absolution?
Freda	You won't provoke me.
Hiker	That's a change!
Freda	Joe's the master here... I'll not go against his wishes. I'm not one to disobey.
Hiker	I was never the master here. I'm resigned to that though.
Freda	You should be resigning yourself to something else now. Will you ever learn?
Hiker	I never learned but one thing and it's too late now to benefit from it. I learned that the shelter of a bush with two people is better than a palace with three. I learned that young couples must finish their fights between themselves and not be running to outsiders when the game gets tough.
Freda	I was never an outsider.
Hiker	I didn't marry you Freda. I married Kate.
Freda	And a good job you made of that.
Hiker	With your help. I wonder if I'd married you, how would it have turned out. The same I'd say.
Freda	I'd never have married you!
Hiker	How do you know? I never asked you. I've a feeling you'd have said 'Yes!' if I proposed to you.

Freda *(Shaken)* How can you behave like this and no
time at all between you and your Maker?

Hiker The truth is bitter!

Freda I never cared in anyway for you, so stop your
foolish talk.

Hiker Your free to go, if you don't want to listen.

Freda *(Outbreak)* Merciful Mother o' God, can't you
leave me alone, can't you? All these years I've
hated you. I was hard and bitter, not like other
women. I was too wise and sober – not like Kate,
she was soft and foolish. I couldn't have ogled
you even if I'd wanted to, it isn't in me. You
came to the house to see the two of us. How
could I know which of us you wanted. When
Kate told me that night that you wanted to marry
her, it was near being the death of me.

Hiker I never gave you any call to think that I was
interested in you, beyond you were Kate's sister.

Freda You did.. you did. You used to rip the strings of
my apron for devilment and you kissed me ... you
kissed me ... you often kissed me.

Hiker That was before I gave my word to Kate. I teased
you and kissed you because you were Kate's sister
and Kate was the girl I loved.

Freda You tricked me. All the talks we had together...

Hiker There was never...

Freda The plans we made, the three of us together,
sitting around the fire at night ... and the places
we went together ... the dances and the hooleys,

the three of us together ... *(Hits the table with her fist fearfully)* but the two of you went off and spoiled all that forever.

Hiker *(Kindly)* That's life Freda. People get married and it's never the same.

(She does not answer, but rises and moves away)

Freda I didn't mean that – I swear to God I didn't.

Hiker You wouldn't let our marriage alone. You wouldn't accept it. I was a man ... I could sport and play and work with the best. I could give and take but this goddamned house was too much for me. I had no one to turn to. I was ashamed to tell my friends that there were two women in my house who wouldn't play their parts ... I was ashamed to say that the women of my house were breaking me between them ... were breaking my pride and spirit because neither was woman enough to face the truth ... that I was no longer a visitor in the house, I was Kate's husband. If it was a man that wronged me I'd have smashed him, but I was striking at air when I tried to break into the secret world of you and Kate. Leaving was a wrong thing to do, it was a heartless thing *(Kate enters on the stairs and stands silently listening to the Hiker)*, and I tried to forget but always in the stillness voices were calling, and the clearest voice was that of my son Joe. My

innocent adoring son that loved me with all his
heart. That was my crime, my most awful crime,
that I killed his wondering innocence when he
needed me most. That night I came back he
struck me – how could I have raised a hand
against him?

(Freda comes to him)

Freda   I'm sorry! I can't say any more. I don't know
how. Just that I'm sorry.

Hiker   We were all to blame – you and me – and Kate
too. She never tried.

Kate   *(Coming down the stairs)* How can you say I never
tried Michael Lacey? ... Eight long years I tried to
keep the peace in this house. Look where it got
me. They say it's hard with three people under the
one roof, unbearable at times. Who knows that
better than you and me and Freda. But other
men made nothing of it. They stayed and they
were loved, but the road was your true love, not
me, *(Joe comes down the stairs into the kitchen)* not
even your children. I can't ever forgive you
Michael. I pity you the way I would pity any sick
thing, and if it's Joe's wish that you should stay
here and be comfortable in your last days I have
no quarrel with that, but it's all I have to give you
and you'll have to make do with it. All right
Michael?

Hiker	All right Kate.
Freda	*(Moving to the stairs)* Goodnight.
Hiker	Goodnight.

(Joe gives way at the stairs to Kate and Freda as they exit, Kate stopping to place a reassuring hand on Joe's arm)

Kate	Goodnight Joe.
Joe	Goodnight mother.

(Kate and Freda exit)

Joe	Your bed is ready whenever you like to go up. I don't know what Mary would think if she found out you were sleeping in her bed.
Hiker	I don't care much what Mary thinks. It's what you think that matters.
Joe	I have to be goin' out ... a few things to do ... check the gates and things .... you'd better go to bed.
Hiker	I'd prefer if we could talk a while.
Joe	Talk? ... What about?
Hiker	Just talk ... I don't know.
Joe	Neither do I.

(Joe takes the whiskey from the sideboard and sits at the table. Pours himself a drink and pushes the bottle over to the Hiker)

Hiker   Death doesn't seem to matter now. It's a powerful thing for a man to have his son near him at the end. *(Pause)* I'd like if you'd bury me near my father in Kilcushna.

Joe   Surely.

Hiker   Things aren't so bad now.

Joe   You shouldn't take much notice of Simey. He's selfish. He only thinks about Simey. He wants to blot you out of his mind altogether ... a hard thing to do.

Hiker   He'll never suceed!

Joe   How do you mean?

Hiker   Oh, he'll be examining a cow someday and he'll ask the owner how old she is and the owner will say: 'I'm not too sure but she was born in the Year of the Hiker!' *(Joe laughs)* Or it might be a horse and the man that owns him will say: 'I bought him, and he a colt, in Cahirmee *(Pause)* the year they buried the Hiker Lacey *(Pause)* the Lord have mercy on him!'

END

MORE MERCIER BESTSELLERS

THREE PLAYS: Sive, The Field, Big Maggie

John B. Keane

SIVE is a powerful folk-drama set in the south-west of Ireland which concerns itself with the attempt of a scheming matchmaker and a bitter woman to sell an innocent young girl to a lecherous old man.

THE FIELD is John B. Keane's fierce and tender study of the love a man can have for land and the ruthless lengths he will go to in order to obtain the object of his desire. *Now a major film.*

BIG MAGGIE: On the death of her husband Maggie is determined to create a better life for herself and her children. The problems arise when her vision of the future begins to sit with increasing discomfort on the shoulders of her surly offspring. John B. Keane's wonderful creation of a rural Irish matriarch ranks with Juno, Mommo and Molly Bloom as one of the great female creations of twentieth-century Irish literature.

THE CHASTITUTE

John B. Keane

'A Chastitute is a person without holy orders who has never lain down with a woman.' This is the definition given by John B. Keane who in this amusing play holds up some 'sacred cows' to ridicule.

MOLL

John B. Keane

An hilariously funny comedy by Ireland's most influential and prolific dramatist

THE MAN FROM CLARE

John B. Keane

The personal tragedy of an aging athlete who finds he no longer has the physical strength to maintain his position as captain of the team or his reputation as the best footballer in Clare.

IRISH SHORT STORIES

John B. Keane

There are more shades to John B. Keane's humour than there are colours in the rainbow. Wit, pathos, compassion, shrewdness and a glorious sense of fun and roguery are seen in this book. This fascinating exploration of the striking yet intangible Irish characteristics show us Keane's sensitivity and deep understanding of everyday life in a rural community.

John B. Keane draws our attention to both the comic and tragic effects of small town gossip in 'The Hanging' — a tale of accusation by silence in a small village — and 'The Change'— a carefully etched comment on a town waking up to undiscovered sexuality. With his natural sense of character, a gift for observing and capturing traits he gives us an hilarious, mischievous and accurate portrait of the balance of justice in 'You're on Next Sunday' and 'A Tale of Two Furs'. We see his uncommon gift for creating characters and atmosphere in 'Death be not Proud' and 'The Fort Field'.

Keane's magic, authentic language and recurrent humour weave their spells over the reader making this exciting book a 'must' for all Keane fans.

LETTERS OF A MATCHMAKER

John B. Keane

The letters of a country matchmaker faithfully recorded by John B. Keane, whose knowledge of matchmaking is second to none.

LETTERS OF A SUCCESSFUL T.D.

John B. Keane

A humorous peep at the correspondence of Tull MacAdoo, a rural Irish parliamentary backbencher.

LETTERS OF AN IRISH PARISH PRIEST

John B. Keane

There is laughter on every page of the correspondence between a country parish priest and his nephew who is studying for the priesthood.

LETTERS OF A LOVE-HUNGRY FARMER

John B. Keane

The story of a man who has never lain with a woman for reasons which are fully disclosed in this book.